NEW KIDS IN AMERICA
- FROM ALL OVER THE WORLD

By Anna Tharp and Lou Tharp
Illustrated By Chris Padovano

Published by Worldwide Children's Books,
New Port Richey, Fl.

First Printing June 2011.

ISBN: 978-0615480275

Printed in the United States of America.

www.worldwidechildrensbooks.com

This book is dedicated to
the millions of kids
around the world who dream
of someday coming to America.
I had the same dreams myself, and
one magic day God made my dreams
come true.

Anna

I would like to dedicate this book to Anna,
who has made
all of my dreams come true, too.

Lou

NEW KIDS IN AMERICA
-FROM ALL OVER THE WORLD

New Kids In America was inspired by author Anna Tharp's observations when she moved from her native Philippines to the United States several years ago. She found the differences in culture and lifestyle fascinating. Anna and her husband Lou Tharp created this book to introduce readers to children from nine different nations who have come to start a new life in America. Children who were born in the USA will come to appreciate how lucky they truly are, as they discover some of the hardships these foreign-born kids have endured.

Each story starts with "HELLO" in the child's native language and ends with their own way of saying "GOODBYE". The reader will see the country's flag, the map of each nation, as well as examples of their money. Enjoy these stories of brave and adventurous children who have left their own country for a better life in America....the land of the free and the home of the brave.

MEXICO
"Hola"

My name is Carlos and I am from Mexico. My ancestors were strong Mayan and Aztec warriors and also brave Spanish bullfighters.

We can work hard and know how to build things. We built huge pyramids almost 2,000 years ago. Today we are building a modern Mexico!

Mexico has the biggest construction company in the world – named Cemex. We build cars, too...in modern factories that use robots. Mexico makes more smart phones than any other country. Some Mexicans are very rich. The richest man in the world this year was a Mexican businessman named Carlos Slim Helu.

Still many of the people are very poor. They work hard, but they do not make much money.
In Mexico it is hard to free yourself from being poor.

Even if some people do not have much money, they know how to have fun. Mexicans love to sing, to dance, and to eat! When I came to the USA, I was happy to see so many Mexican restaurants. People here seem to love our tacos and burritos.

Many Americans come to visit Mexico every year because it has beautiful beaches and good fishing!

MEXICO

"Adios"

My father says that America is our new home, so we need to learn its language and its customs. Of course, we still keep many of our Mexican customs! When I had a birthday party, I invited my new American friends and showed them how to break open a piñata. It is full of candy! Now they all want a piñata at their next birthday party!

My father says that in America anyone who works hard is free to become anything they want to be. I want to own a Mexican restaurant that will have musicians and dancers and the best tacos in town!

PHILIPPINES
"Kumusta"

I was born in Cebu, one of the largest of the 7,107 islands in my country. My mother named me Rinalyn, but my friends call me Lynn.
I was the baby of a big family.
I have three older sisters and
three older brothers.

My father had a hard time trying to feed all nine of us. On some nights there was no food to eat except a little rice. Even though we were so poor, we were still happy – and hard working. My father taught us to always tell the truth and to love our family.

My father's dream was to see all
of his children happily married.
My sister, Marisa, married a very
nice man named Michael. Marisa
looked so beautiful and she let me
carry her flowers.

My father was a "jeepney" bus driver.
He had to work 10 hours every day. He was
paid 500 pesos a day. That is about twelve
dollars in American money. His only day off
was Sundays, so we all went to church.

I was very happy growing up in the Philippines. The Philippines has so many beautiful beaches. I liked to swim and to sail on the fast native boats.

I also loved the fiesta times. The church in each village holds many festivals and parades.

One time my sister and my brother were the king and queen. The girls liked to dress up for village beauty contests. We dreamed to maybe become Miss Philippines. Many boys hoped to become a prize fighter, like Manny "Pac Man" Pacquiao – our world champion.

PHILIPPINES
"Paalam Na"

I really loved school! Sometimes it was hard for my parents to have enough money to send me. School is free, but you have to have money for paper and for lunch. Filipino parents are so happy when their children graduate. When my oldest brother finished college, he got a job and started giving my mother money so she could go back to college at night. In a few years, my mom became a nurse.

That is how we came to America! My mother applied for a nursing job in a hospital in Florida. The hospital paid for her, my father, and me to come to the USA. When we got to America, I could not believe my eyes! Almost everyone has a car here! Back home, very few own a car. Now we have bought a little car and we are saving to buy a house. They also can send some money back to help their grandkids. Everyone helps each other in the Philippines. We are one big happy family!

CUBA
"Hola"

Hola! My name is Mario and I was born on the island of Cuba! Cuba is a beautiful country with lots of beaches.

We are a happy people who love to have fun – dancing, singing, eating, and playing sports. Baseball is my favorite.

Cuba is only 90 miles from the south tip of Florida. Even though we are so close, Cuba is very different than America! Over 50 years ago, a man named Fidel Castro turned Cuba into a communist country. Castro made himself a dictator which means that he is the boss of all Cuba.

After Castro took over, our country has become very poor. We only have old cars now. Everyone is afraid of Castro's police and his army. If you say something against the government, they may put you in jail.

My father decided that we must leave Cuba and escape to America. Castro will not let anyone leave the island, but some are brave enough to try to cross the dangerous seas. Secretly, my father and two uncles began to build a small raft made of rubber inner tubes and scrap wood. Then one dark night we carried our homemade boat to the beach and pushed it into the water.
It was so scary!

We paddled all night hoping the police patrol boats would not spot us. For nine days we hung on to our raft. Sometimes sharks would come and circle around us. We grew tired, sunburned, and almost out of food and water. Then, suddenly one morning we saw land! We all started shouting and paddling hard until we reached a beach. Some people ran over to help us pull our raft up on the sand. We had landed in America!
Soon a police car came up. I was afraid when I saw them, but they were nice to us. One of the policemen gave me a cold drink and my first American hot dog!

CUBA

"Adiós"

Now I am going to school in Miami and we are all proud to be Cuban-Americans! What I love most about America is that the police are your friends. You do not have to be afraid of them. When I grow up I want to be an American policeman.

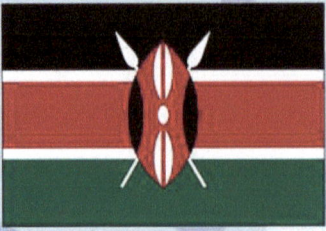

KENYA

"Jambo"

My name is Matu. I grew up in Kenya in Africa. If you like animals, you would love my country. You can see elephants, giraffes, zebras, and even lions. I lived in Nairobi, our biggest city, but just by walking outside of town, you can see wild animals.

Once I was surprised when I saw an elephant on the dirt road right in front of me. I took off running, before he might charge at me.

We are fast runners in Kenya! My hero is Kenya's famous runner named Rudisha. He is a world champion.

When I came to school in America, the teacher let us all run a race. I was the winner.

She asked me how I learned to run so fast. I said, "By running away from elephants!"

The schools in America are so nice! You get a desk of your own and your own book to read. In many schools in Kenya the desks are old and you have to share the books. Our classroom was always hot, because Kenya is at the equator! Some children are too poor to go to school. I was very lucky because my father was a college teacher and he made sure I went to school and studied hard.

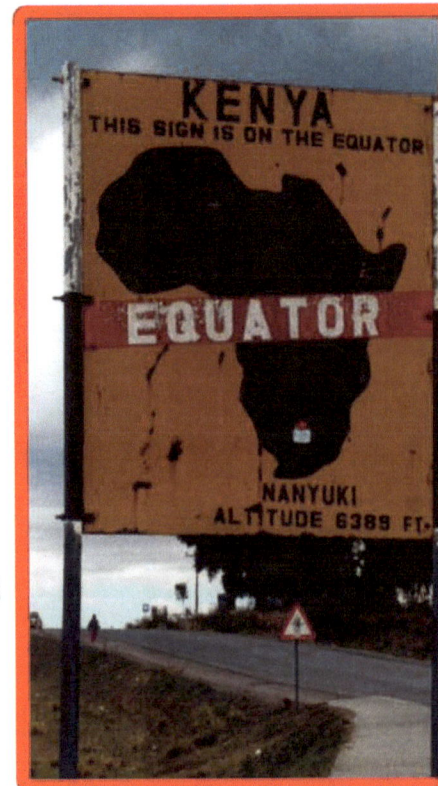

KENYA
"Alamsiki"

My father was so smart that a college named Harvard asked him to come to teach here in America. President Obama's father came from Kenya, too, and he was once a student at Harvard. So Predisent Obama is also a big hero of mine—next to Rudisha! If they ran a race, I bet Rudisha would win. I am just kidding!

In Kenya, we do not worry about who is faster, or smarter, or richer.
Our national motto is one word: "Harambee!" In our Swahili language it means "Let's all pull together." Father says Americans think like that, too. That why when I pledge allegiance to my new American flag, we all say: "*one nation, under God, with liberty and justice for all.*" It means Harambee!

ENGLAND

"Alright Mate"

I was born in London, England, the capitol of the United Kingdom. My name is Elizabeth, just like our Queen, but everyone calls me "Liz".

England is a beautiful country with lots of history. We have many castles where famous kings and queens have lived. I liked to watch the marching guards at Buckingham Palace.

My father was a banker and was always busy working to make a lot of money. One week he flew to America for a business meeting. When he came back, he told us that he wanted to move to Texas and buy a ranch!

What a surprise! My mother and I did not like the idea of leaving city life in London to go live out in the country with a bunch of cows!

Daddy said, "Come with me on a visit to America and see what you think."

From the first day I fell in love with Texas! The kids were so friendly and we had so much fun. We rode horses and camped out in the fields. My mother was having fun, too. I saw her kissing daddy while they were sitting on a fence.

The next day they asked me, "Do you want to move to America?" I said, "Whoopee!", a new American word I learned. So my father bought a big ranch and hired over 20 American cowboys to help us run it.

ENGLAND

"Laters"

He sold his Rolls Royce car in London. Now he drives a new truck!
I ride a horse to school! School is easy, because I already speak English. Sometimes the kids laugh at my "English accent," but I don't care. We are all friends!
Once the teacher told the class, "The English invented English, you know – and Liz speaks it perfectly!"

I love my teacher and I love living in Texas. Now I even love the cows, but they *do* stink!

SOUTH KOREA
안녕
(Hello-"annyeong")

My name is Kim and I came from South Korea. Korea is a mixture of the old and the very new. We honor our elders and use their wisdom to leap ahead into the future. You will see many beautiful Buddhist temples in our country, right next to modern buildings.

Koreans like to try the newest things – like smart phones, computerized classrooms, and the most modern cars.

My dad designs cars for Hyundai. Hyundai and the Kia cars are made in Korea.

My parents taught me to try my very best at everything I do. Koreans learn to study hard, work hard, and even fight hard! When I was only four, I started to learn Taekwondo! That is the name of our Korean fighting style. It is taught here in America, too. In 2004, Jang Ji-won, a Korean girl, won the Olympic gold medal in Taekwondo. Someday I hope I can kick as high as she can.

In the Korean schools we had to compete very hard for good grades. Our classroom was even more modern than the American school I go to now. Each of us had our own computer and the teacher had a big screen monitor.

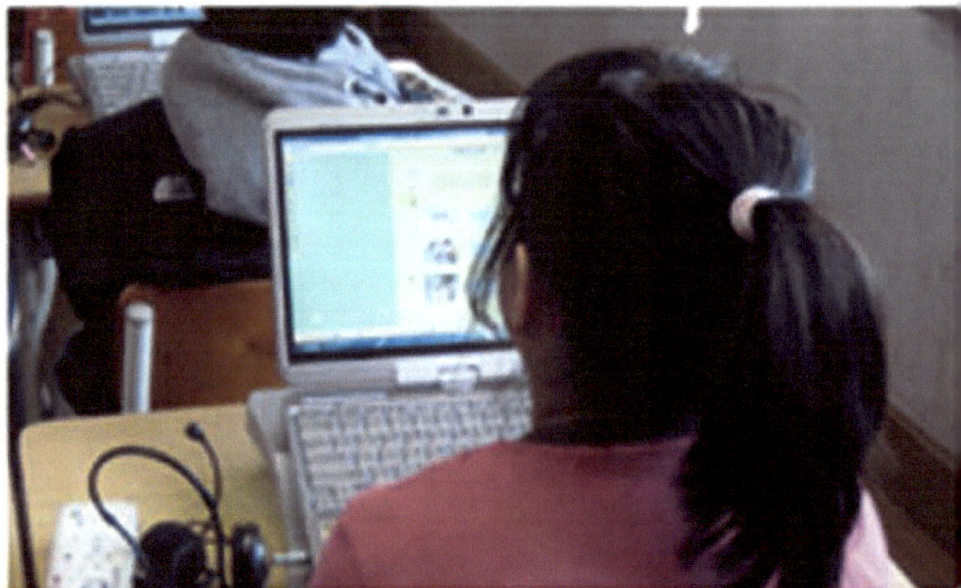

SOUTH KOREA

안녕 히 가십시오

(Goodbye- "Annyeong hi gasipsio")

After a long day studying, we would walk home together - and then do three hours of homework! Maybe that is why I am already ahead of my American classmates in math and in science.

"English is a Very Hard Subject"

영어는 매우 어려운 피사체

("Yeong-eoneun maeu eolyeoun pisache")

English is my hardest subject, because our language in Korea is so different. We use characters instead of letters. It is not easy to pronounce some English words, but I will keep trying. My father says that we Koreans never give up. My dream is to be an honor student in every subject – even in English! I want to be a success in my new country, America!

CHINA

你好

(Hello—"Nǐ hǎo")

My name is Hu and I came here from China. China has the most people of any nation in the world – over one billion and three hundred million people! That is four times as many people as live in the USA. Imagine that every time you saw an American, there were four more Chinese people standing next to them.

Just 30 years ago, China was very poor, but then we began to build thousands of new factories. Everywhere you look in China a new building is going up.

The Chinese workers set a world record by building a complete 15-story hotel in just six days. China also built the fastest train in the world. It can go 302 miles per hour.

You might think the Chinese people are rich, but most are still poor. The reason is that there are so many people – crowded into small apartments. Most factory workers only make about $100 a month. Only a few rich people have a car. Most just use a bicycle to ride to work or school.

In China we have great respect for our parents and our teachers. When our teachers would walk into the classroom, we would all stand up to honor them. We honor our ancestors, too – with statues and temples. Centuries ago they built China's Great Wall. They have all struggled hard to give China a bright new future.

CHINA
好
(Goodbye- "Liánghǎo de")

When I came to America, I was surprised that life is so easy here. The American houses are so big and many families have two cars – and a garage! The garage in our American house is as big as our whole apartment was in China!

58201 68012 0
MADE IN CHINA

I love the American malls! The stores are so full of things to buy, but I saw that almost every one of them had a label – "Made in China". I am studying hard to someday become rich and build my own factory to make things stamped "Made in USA" – by a Chinese American! Me!

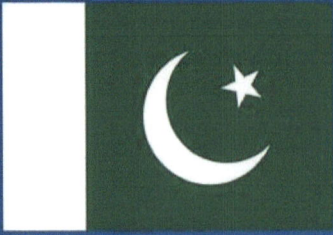

PAKISTAN
"Assalam-o-Alekum"

My name is Aisha and I was born in Pakistan. Pakistan is a beautiful country with many high mountains. One is named K2. It is the second highest mountain in the world. Hikers come from all over the world to try to climb to the top.

We love beautiful colors in our clothes and even our buses.

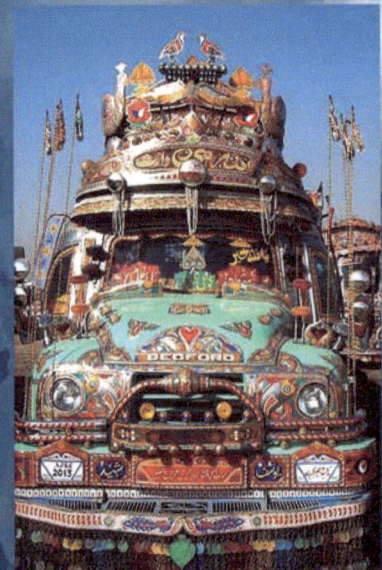

Our religion is called Islam and we pray 5 times every day. In Pakistan we had special prayer rooms everywhere you go – in school, in the office buildings, even in gas stations.

Our Muslim religious buildings are called mosques. People gather at the mosque on Friday to pray to Allah. Allah is our name for God.

In the cities, we have some very tall new buildings, but many people living in the country are poor. Some children cannot learn how to read and write because their village may not have a school. We girls loved to read books when we had a chance.

One year we had a big flood and over a million people lost their house. The movie star Angelina Jolie visited Pakistan to help us. She wore a scarf out of respect for our religion.

Many Pakistani ladies like to wear a scarf, so only their husband can see their pretty hair. You do not have to wear it. My oldest sister joined the Pakistani Army and she wears a soldier's cap.

PAKISTAN
"Khuda-hafiz"

When I started school in the United States, no one was wearing a scarf except me. Some of the others students pointed at me, and didn't understand why I wore a scarf. My teacher understood and came in the next day wearing a pretty scarf too. It was her way to make me feel welcome. She said that in America everyone has freedom of religion. I love America! You are free to be whatever you want to be.

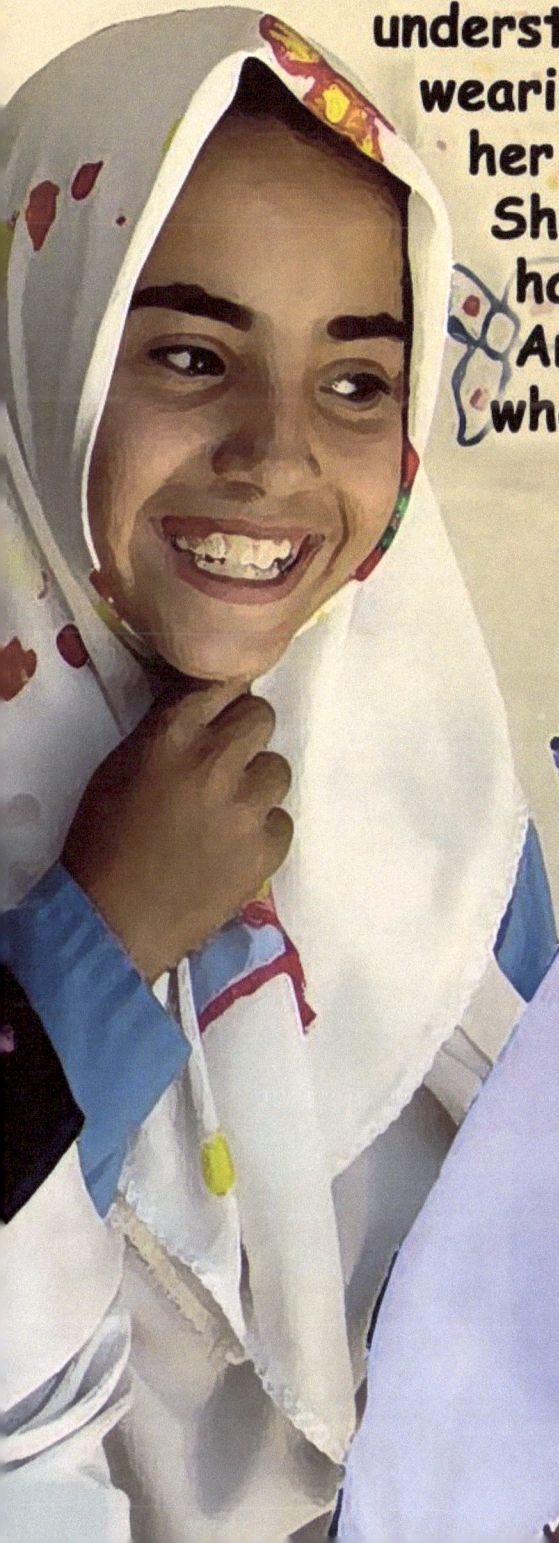

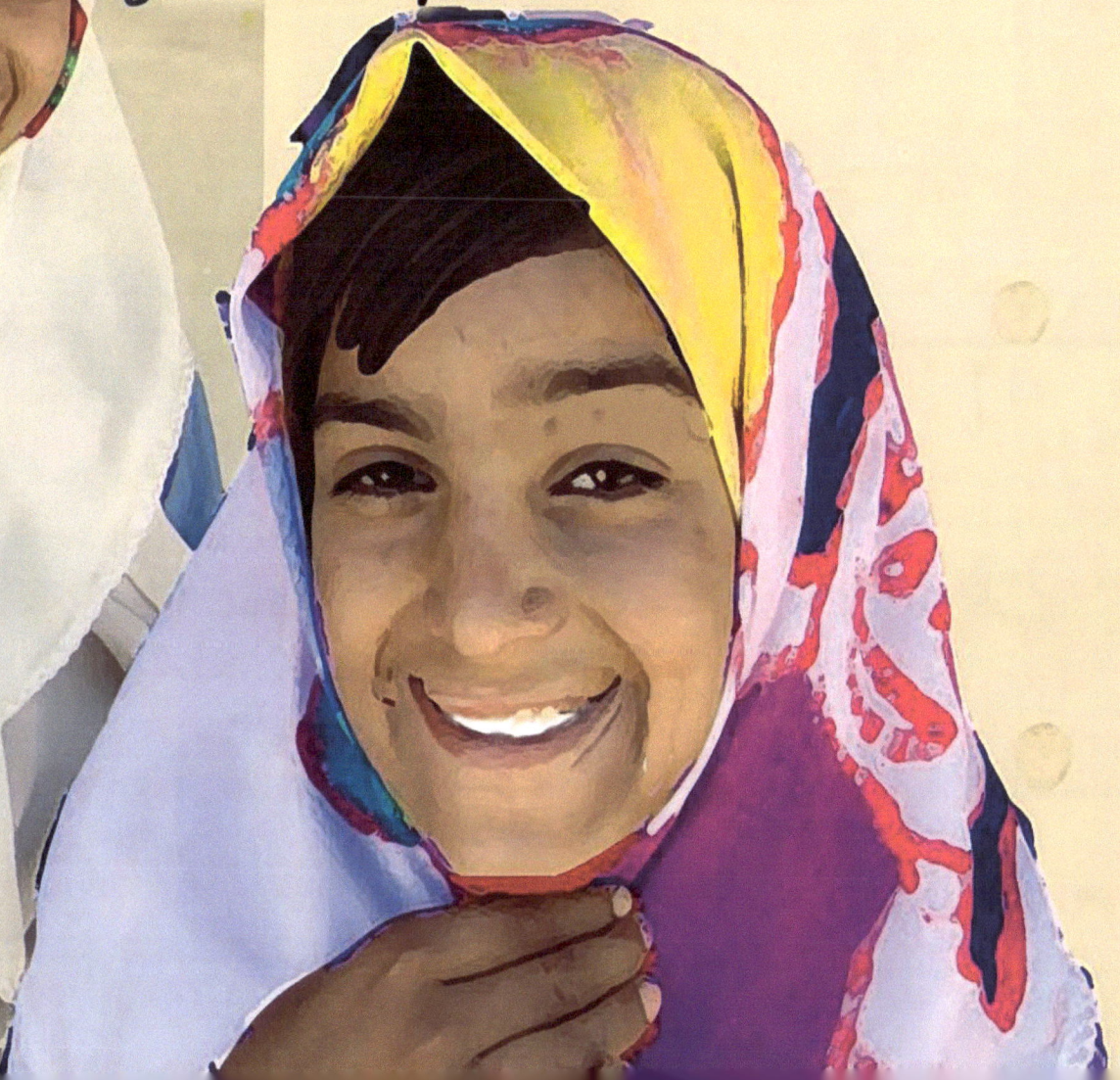

INDIA
"Namastē"

My name is Seema and I am from India. We are a big country with over a billion people. We used to live in a big city called Mumbai. It is where they make Indian movies, so they call it Bollywood – like the American Hollywood!

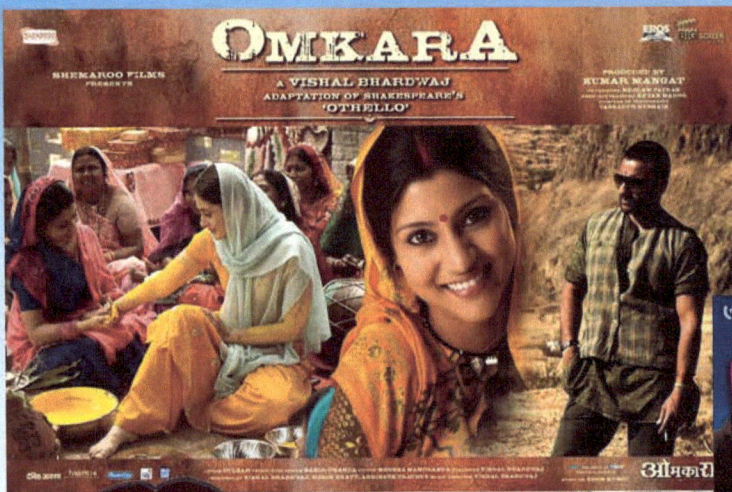

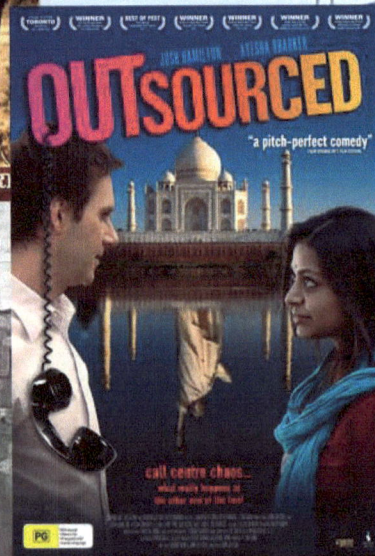

Bollywood makes even more movies every year than they do in the U.S. Our movie stars speak Hindi, which is our national language. Almost everyone in India can also speak very good English.

That is why many American companies hire us to answer telephone calls from Americans to help them with things, like maybe their cell phone. India has more cell phones than any country in the world. That is because we have so many people! Many may be poor but they are still happy.

The most important thing to Indian people is not money! It is our family! That is why weddings are very special times in India. The bride and groom dress up in fancy clothes and honor many old customs. A marriage brings together not only two souls, but also the two families.

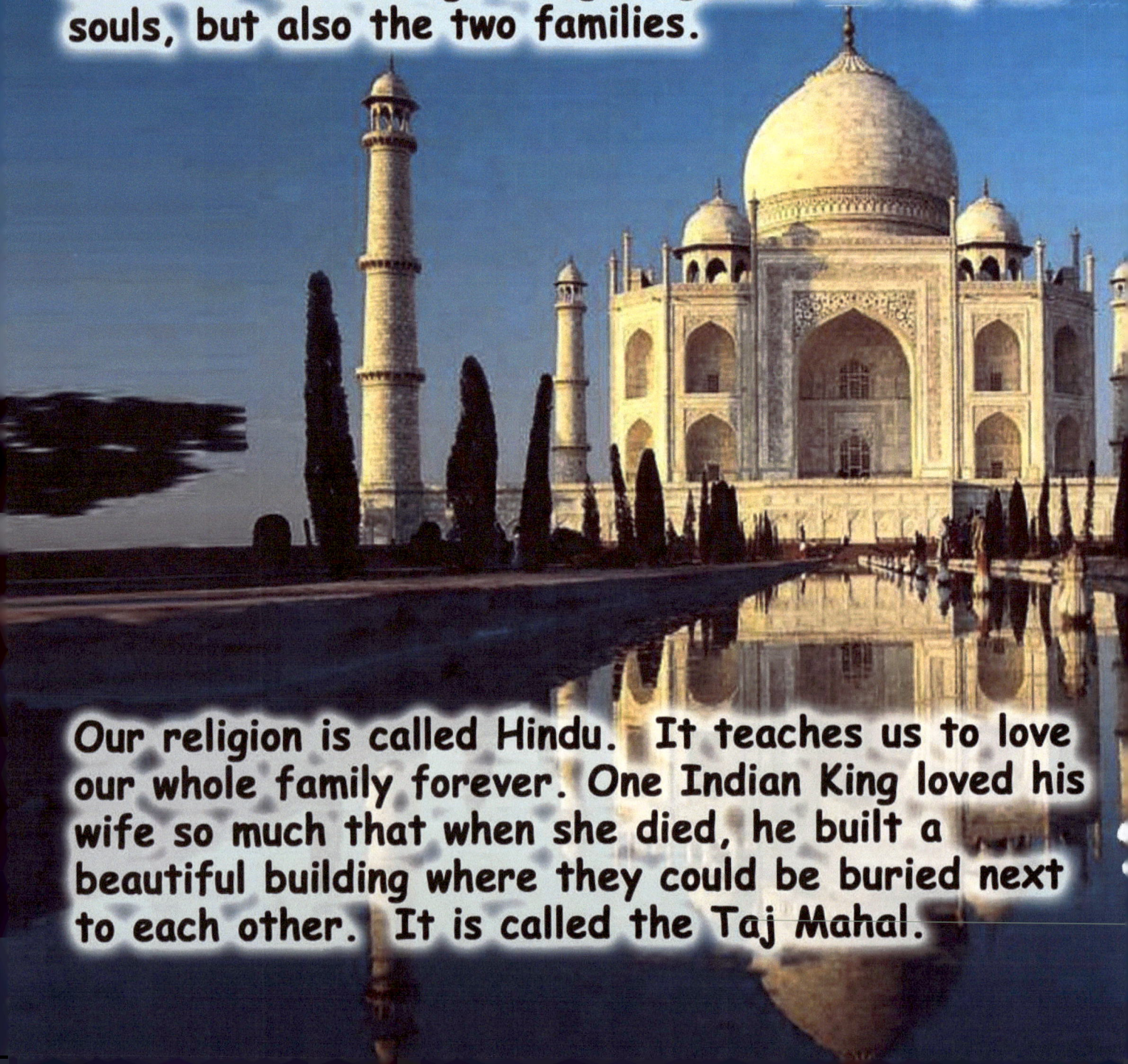

Our religion is called Hindu. It teaches us to love our whole family forever. One Indian King loved his wife so much that when she died, he built a beautiful building where they could be buried next to each other. It is called the Taj Mahal.

INDIA

"Accha Namastē"

Our most famous national hero was a man named Mahatma Gandhi. He taught us how to gain freedom without using guns. His ways have been used all over the world, even in America.

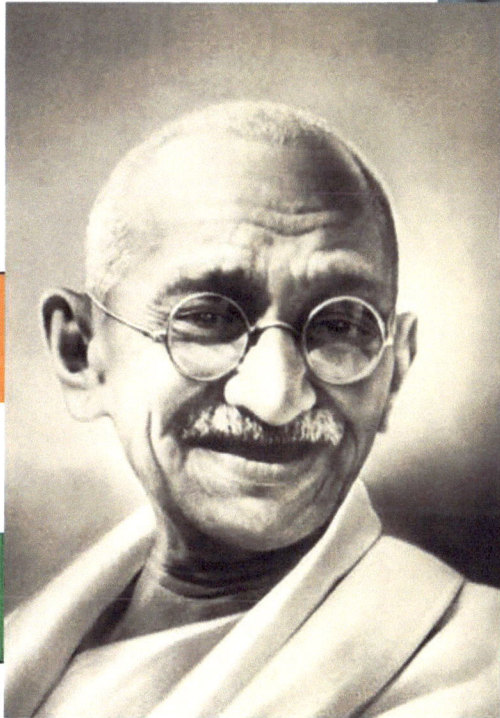

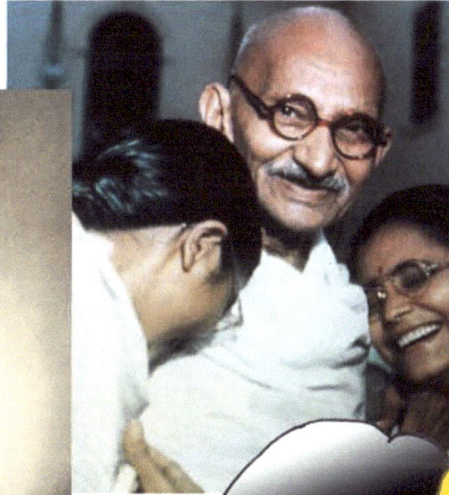

We came to the USA to work for my uncle who owns a motel. We live in the motel so I get to meet kids from all over the United States. Americans are so friendly! They tell me about the places they come from and I tell them about India. When I grow up I am going to get a car and take a long trip to see everything in America, my new country.

WE NEED 22 MORE BOOKS!

The new kids in America come from over 200 nations! This book only tells about kids from a few. Look at the list on the next page! If we told a story about ALL of the countries are sending people to the United States, we would need to write 22 more books! For over 400 years, people from all over the world have bravely traveled to make their new home in America. All of these millions have freely come together in one nation, each bringing their own strengths and talents. United, they have built the strongest country in the world. These new kids are proud to become a part of "the land of the free, and the home of the brave".

NEW KIDS IN AMERICA COME FROM OVER 200 NATIONS

Afghanistan
Albania
Algeria
Andorra
Angola
Antigua and Barbuda
Argentina
Armenia
Australia
Austria
Azerbaijan
Bahamas
Bahrain
Bangladesh
Barbados
Belarus
Belgium
Belize
Benin
Bhutan
Bolivia
Bosnia and Herzegovina
Botswana
Brazil
Brunei
Bulgaria
Burkina Faso
Burma
Burundi
Cambodia
Cameroon
Canada
Cape Verde
Central African Republic
Chad
Chile
China
Colombia

Comoros
Congo (Brazzaville)
Congo (Kinshasa)
Costa Rica
Cote d'Ivoire
Croatia
Cuba
Cyprus
Czech Republic
Denmark
Djibouti
Dominica
Dominican Republic
East Timor
Ecuador
Egypt
El Salvador
Equatorial Guinea
Eritrea
Estonia
Ethiopia
Fiji
Finland
France
Gabon
Gambia
Georgia
Germany
Ghana
Greece
Grenada
Guatemala
Guinea
Guinea-Bissau
Guyana
Haiti
Holy See
Honduras
Hong Kong
Hungary
Iceland

India
Indonesia
Iran
Iraq
Ireland
Israel
Italy
Jamaica
Japan
Jordan
Kazakhstan
Kenya
Kiribati
Korea, North
Korea, South
Kosovo
Kuwait
Kyrgyzstan
Laos
Latvia
Lebanon
Lesotho
LiberiaLibya
Liechtenstein
Lithuania
Luxembourg
Macau
Macedonia
Madagascar
Malawi
Malaysia
Maldives
Mali
Malta
Marshall Islands
Mauritania
Mauritius
Mexico
Micronesia
Moldova
Monaco

Mongolia
Montenegro
Morocco
Mozambique
Namibia
Nauru
Nepal
Netherlands
Netherlands Antilles
New Zealand
Nicaragua
Niger
Nigeria
Norway
Oman
Pakistan
Palau
Palestinian Territories
Panama
Papua New Guinea
Paraguay
Peru
Philippines
Poland
Portugal
Qatar
Romania
Russia
Rwanda
Saint Kitts and Nevis
Saint Lucia
Saint Vincent and the Grenadines
Samoa
San Marino
Sao Tome and Principe
Saudi Arabia
Senegal
Serbia

Seychelles
Sierra Leone
Singapore
Slovakia
Slovenia
Solomon Islands
Somalia
South Africa
Spain
Sri Lanka
Sudan
Suriname
Swaziland
Sweden
Switzerland
Syria
Taiwan
Tajikistan
Tanzania
Thailand
Timor-Leste
Togo
Tonga
Trinidad and Tobago
Tunisia
Turkey
Turkmenistan
Tuvalu
Uganda
Ukraine
United Arab Emirates
United Kingdom
Uruguay
Uzbekistan
Vanuatu
Venezuela
Vietnam
Yemen
Zambia
Zimbabwe